I WANT TO MAKE ONE THING PERFECTLY CLEAR

I WANT TO MAKE ONE THING PERFECTLY CLEAR

The Illuminations of Richard M. Nixon

compiled by Amram M. Ducovny

illustrations by Peter Green

Ballantine Books · New York
An Intext Publisher

SBN 345-02690-X-100

First Printing: December, 1971

Second Printing: March, 1972

Printed in the United States of America

BALLANTINE BOOKS, INC.
101 Fifth Avenue, New York, N.Y. 10003

For Checkers

Now You See Them . . . Now You Don't:

For example, Senator Aiken, Senator Mansfield—I see him virtually every two or three weeks for breakfast.

March 22, 1971, 10:16 P.M. EST

I eat breakfast alone, never have any guests for lunch—I do that in five minutes, too.

March 22, 1971, 10:17 P.M. EST

So There!

The president must bear in mind the distinction between forceful leadership and stubborn willfulness.

September 19, 1968

I'm not afraid of anybody. I'm not afraid of any audience. I'm not afraid of any press conference. So that's the way it's going to be and don't plant any words in my mouth.

September 27, 1968

Glorioski:

The president's chief function is to lead.

September 19, 1968

I always feel just a little bit embarrassed when an admiral comes up to me and says, "Sir." I think it should be the other way around.

January 31, 1969

The One or Two or Three or Four China Policy:

I call on Adlai Stevenson to renounce his previously expressed ideas and declare unequivocally that he opposes recognition of Red China and supports free China. . . . Unless he does this, he forfeits the right to even be considered for the presidency.

October 29, 1952

I cannot say whether the United States will ever recognize Red China.

July 10, 1956

There are some who tell us that from a practical business standpoint we are foolish to persist in our refusal to recognize Red China and to admit its representatives to the United Nations. But the executive and legislative branches of our government have flatly rejected cowardly expediency in this matter.

September 7, 1956

Dealing with Red China is something like trying to cope with the more explosive ghetto elements in our own country . . . in neither case can we afford to let those now self-exiled from society stay exiled forever.

October 1, 1967

The policy of this country and this administration at this time will be to continue to oppose Communist China's admission to the UN.

January 27, 1969

We have taken two steps [toward] a more normal relationship with mainland China . . . This we think is a goal well worth pursuing.

June 7, 1971

Our action in seeking a new relationship with the People's Republic of China will not be at the expense of old friends.

July 19, 1971

1. XY-yes
2. AB-NO
3. ZK-NO
MAYBE
4 ZB-YES
5 XZ-NO

Will the Real Harry Truman Stand Up?

In the administration around Harry Truman are crooks and incompetents. Truman is among the incompetents.

October 10, 1952

I think it is important to point out that without your [Truman's] leadership of the United States and the free world setting up this great [NATO] Alliance, we would not have had the strength which has avoided a world war since that time.

March 21, 1969

Stumbling Through History:

I'm in next week now.

September 29, 1956

Where am I?

September 30, 1956

But the CIA is not supposed to be here.

March 7, 1969

I am in the wrong place. It says *Miami Convention Center.*

November 7, 1970

No! No! A Million Times Yes!

We are not considering wage or price controls.

October 17, 1969

Permanent wage and price controls in America would stifle the American economy, its dynamism, its productivity, and would be . . . a mortal blow to the U.S. as a first-class economic power.

August 9, 1971

I am today ordering a freeze on all prices and wages for a period of ninety days.

August 21, 1971

As far as the duration of Phase II [of wage-price controls] is concerned, we are not going to set a limit on it.

September 27, 1971

Come to Me, My Schizophrenic Baby:

I am today imposing an additional tax of ten percent on all goods imported to the U.S.

August 21, 1971

This nation is not going to turn inward. We are not going to build protective walls to shelter us from competition.

September 13, 1971

Bad Mouth—Good Mouth:

America's prestige abroad will be just as high as spokesmen for America permit it to be. Now when we have a presidential candidate stating over and over that the U.S. is second in the space race . . . that we have the worst slums . . . that 17 million people go to bed hungry every night; when he makes statements like these, what does this do to American prestige?

October 21, 1960

Our example has lost its fire. Our leadership has lost its drive. The world has lost respect for our judgement, its faith in our ideal, its confidence in our dollar, its trust in our word.

November 19, 1968

Prejudice Can Be Beautiful:

We cannot have construction unions which deny the right of all Americans to have those positions.

September 26, 1969

The hardhat will stand as a symbol, along with our great flag, for freedom and patriotism to our beloved country.

May 5, 1970

Forget Me Not, Remember:

He typifies the truth of the statement that in America there is no forgotten man . . .

October 18, 1956

It is the voice of the great majority of Americans, the forgotten Americans . . .

August 7, 1968

What Did He Say, Hans?

There have been some changes in Washington in recent months. For example, the Washington Redskins have a new coach, Vince Lombardi . . . the Washington Senators have a new manager, Ted Williams . . .

Opening remarks in West Berlin, February 27, 1969

See How Easy It Is?

HOWARD K. SMITH: I think in your press conference you said that traffic on the Ho Chi Minh Trail had been cut by fifty-five percent. The same day the UPI quoted the military command in Saigon as saying it had been cut only twenty percent, which is quite a drastic difference. Can you match those?

PRESIDENT NIXON: Yes. The military commander in Saigon was actually completely correct and so was I.

March 22, 1971

What, Never?

Adlai E. Stevenson holds a Ph.D. degree from Dean Acheson's College of Cowardly Communist Containment.

October 9, 1952

I have no apologies . . . because throughout my career I have campaigned only on issues, never on personalities.

October 23, 1968

See How to Cool It:

You see these bums, you know, blowing up campuses.

May 1, 1970

I would hope that all members of this administration would have in mind the fact—a rule that I have always had, and it is a very simple one—when the action is hot, keep the rhetoric cool.

May 8, 1970

This historic house has witnessed many historic occasions but . . . no visit to this house has greater historic significance. . . .

July 8, 1969

This is a very historic occasion. . . .

July 11, 1969

This is an historic occasion.

August 2, 1969

Before we make some of the official rewards on this historic occasion . . .

August 13, 1969

As I am sure most of you realize, this is an historic occasion.

August 21, 1969

As I stand on this historic site . . .

September 8, 1969

This is your third visit to the United States, but this is indeed a historic day.

November 19, 1969

This is really a very historic occasion for this house. . . .

November 27, 1969

Sweepings:

I pledge that a Nixon administration will sweep the streets of Washington clean of these marauders and criminals and remove from this city the atmosphere of apprehension and fear that hangs over it.

June 22, 1968

I wish I could report that we had produced a magic formula that would end crime [in Washington] and sweep away despair overnight. We have not.

January 31, 1969

D.C.
SANITA
DEPT

Unequal Opportunity = Equal Opportunity:

I do not subscribe to the general view that in this country it is essential that we work toward . . . a country in which there is equal opportunity for education, for employment and in which all the good things of this life are guaranteed all citizens regardless of race, creed or color.

September 26, 1956

Black Americans . . . want an equal chance to own their own homes, to own their own businesses, to be managers and executives. . . . I pledge to you tonight that we shall have new programs which will provide an equal chance.

August 8, 1968

$E = mc^2$

Then you have two Secretaries of State. You cannot have that, there being only one.

March 22, 1971

Second Class Greatness:

I can tell you, as one who has visited over sixty countries in the world, I think every people in this world is a great people, and a great country. If we think that way, we are going to go a long way.

July 22, 1969

They are lucky to be born in the United States. Anyone who has a choice in the world would not choose any other country but the United States. Never let them forget it.

December 3, 1969

May I Introduce Your Friendly CIA Agent:

The United States cannot afford to have an espionage lack or lag.

October 13, 1960

We extend the hand of friendship to all people. To the Russian people. To the Chinese people. And we shall work toward the goal of an open world, open sky, open cities, open minds.

August 8, 1968

Open and Shut:

This is an open administration. It will continue to be so.

May 5, 1970

You can still ask the questions, but I may not give answers.

January 4, 1971

Here Don't Come the Judge:

I think when we judge whether this operation [Laos] is going to be labeled a success or failure, we cannot judge it before it is concluded, and we cannot judge it even after it is concluded.

March 22, 1971

Promise Them Anything:

In the Nixon administration students . . . are going to have a piece of the action.

September 9, 1968

I understand there has been and continues to be opposition to the war in Vietnam on the campuses. . . . We expect it. However, under no circumstances will I be affected by it.

September 26, 1969

Grace Under Pressure:

Let me say this: I don't believe that I ought to quit, because I'm no quitter.

September 20, 1952

But as I leave you—just think how much you are going to miss me. You won't have Nixon to kick around anymore.

November 8, 1962

How High Above?

The Supreme Court has given the green light to criminal elements.

May 8, 1968

Crime, respect for law, dealing with crime, these are issues above partisan politics.

June 11, 1970

And, Two Wars Later . . .

President Eisenhower's leadership will serve to avoid armed conflict in the Middle East.

October 13, 1956

Well, the situation in the Middle East has become ominous due to the fact that reports have been received with regard to Soviet pilots being interjected into the U.A.R. Air Force.

May 11, 1970

Perhaps a Chapter:

Perhaps I should take a leaf out of the book of a man [Truman] who spoke last night and indulge in some name-calling. But I know I can't equal him in name-calling.

October 12, 1952

I charge that the buried record will show that Mr. Truman and his associates, either through stupidity or political expedience, were primarily responsible for the unimpeded growth of the Communist conspiracy in the United States.

October 18, 1952

Thanks for the Shaft:

I did not win. I have no hard feelings against anyone.

November 8, 1962

If they [the press] are against a candidate, give him the shaft, but also recognize if they give him the shaft, put one lonely reporter on the campaign who will report what the candidate says now and then.

November 8, 1962

You Are Humbly Fired:

I am sure Secretary Hickel will assume the great responsibility to see that his president also remains humble.

January 24, 1969

The problem of confidence when you have a cabinet team . . . is something that can't really be described that precisely . . . I thought when I appointed Mr. Hickel that we would have mutual confidence. . . . Under the circumstances I thought a change was right.

December 10, 1970

It Depends on Whose Pie Is in the Sky:

Our hope is to double everyone's standard of living in ten years.

September 23, 1956

A president must tell the people what cannot be done immediately as well as what can. . . . America needs charts of the possible, not excursions into the impossible.

September 19, 1968

Dick Nixon, Everywhere, Everyman:

I am a resident of Washington.

February 13, 1969

Mrs. Nixon's father was Irish and on my side my mother was Irish. So between us you have one.

March 17, 1969

I was born in the little town of Yorba Linda.

April 14, 1969

I feel at home here [Madison, South Dakota].

June 3, 1969

Thanks for this wonderful welcome to my home county, Orange County.

July 15, 1969

. . . my wife, whose mother was born in Germany, and our two daughters who are therefore one fourth German.

August 7, 1969

At the Parliament in Bonn, she [Mrs. Nixon] could say: "This is not my fatherland, but it is my mother's land."

August 7, 1969

I am the only Quaker in the room.

October 22, 1969

It's good to be back home in Indiana.

October 20, 1970

I also own property in Florida.

October 27, 1970

I speak to you as a former Virginian.

October 28, 1970

What a proud moment it is for me to be addressing the nation . . . from my home state of California.

October 30, 1970

I was raised on Arizona's water.

October 31, 1970

Be Independent When You Say "Yes":

I don't want a government of yes-men, but one in which dissenters will get a hearing . . . and one in which there will be a true ferment of ideas.

September 20, 1968

I want a Secretary of State that will join me in cleaning house in the State Department . . . It's going to be a Nixon-oriented State Department.

October 23, 1968

Advanced Semantics:

Now, what was wrong? And let me say that it was wrong—I'm saying, incidentally that it was wrong and not just illegal. Because it isn't a question of whether it was legal or illegal. That isn't enough. The question is: was it morally wrong.

September 20, 1952

Maybe Give a Little:

We will never engage in a policy of international give-away.

October 10, 1956

The United States should not take the responsibility in the future to send American men in to defend the neutrality of countries that are unable to defend themselves.

May 8, 1970

The Deductive Mind at Work:

PRESIDENT NIXON: Where are you going to college?

PERRY LUDY (*Boys Club "Boy of the Year"*): I am interested in pre-med.

PRESIDENT NIXON: You are going to be a doctor, perhaps?

March 19, 1969

And on the Seventh Day . . .

I want this nation to be at peace and we shall be. I want the air to be clean and it will be clean. I want the water to be pure and it will be pure. I want better education for all Americans . . . and that shall be.

May 28, 1970

When I say *I* have, I shouldn't use that in such a, shall we say, arrogant fashion.

March 22, 1971

Inner Peace! Inner Peace, I Say!

For once, Gentlemen [the press], I would appreciate it if you would write what I say. . . . I think it is very important that you write it in the lead—*in the lead.*

November 8, 1962

The most important single factor is that he [the president] must be one who has perspective and poise, what the Quakers call peace at the center, one who isn't knocked out of balance by the stories, the crises of the moment, one who having that peace at the center then will make decisions with regard . . . to the lives of men . . . in a way that will be in the best interests of the country.

March 22, 1971

And Then I'll Tuck You in Beddy-Bye:

We are going to get up early and work late and do everything we can so this [White] house will always be a happy house and your home will always be a happy home.

January 24, 1969

There's Trust and Trust:

Under no circumstances must the United States make an agreement [on control of nuclear weapons] on trust.

October 13, 1960

We signed the Nuclear Nonproliferation Treaty prompted in the fervent hope that this decision would contribute to . . . mutual trust among nations.

February 27, 1969

Sometimes You Can Be Too Profound:

I think you reach young people more by talking to them as adults . . . I like to treat them as adults. I like to talk to them.

December 9, 1969

I told them [students] that in 1939 I thought Neville Chamberlain was the greatest man living and Winston Churchill was a madman. It was not until years later that I realized Chamberlain was a good man, but Churchill was right. I doubt if that got over.

May 9, 1970

Consistency:

In many cases, religious schools are performing indispensable community services and would seem to merit public support.

October 31, 1968

I happen to believe that the Constitution should be strictly interpreted.

May 22, 1969

Help, Help! Don't You Dare!

Neither the U.S. nor the Soviet Union will submit their interests to a vote of over one-hundred nations, many of whom do not have the same responsibilities, for example, as we have.

December 20, 1968

This makes it urgent that the UN members, those in this room who have taken an active interest in peace in Vietnam, now take an active hand in achieving it.

September 18, 1969

Next Question?

I recognize that is an intriguing question. I probably have a very good answer. . . . Ask me next year at this time and I will give you an answer.

March 22, 1971

What Are They Still Doing There?

Out of the turmoil in the Middle East will come a more stable area in which the Soviet Union will not be a decisive influence.

November 2, 1956

In the Middle East talks, we have not seen on the Soviet side that practical and constructive flexibility which is necessary for a successful outcome, and without which the responsibility of the great powers in the search for a settlement cannot be met.

February 23, 1970

Zig, Zag, Zig:

Know your enemy for what he is: a godless, ruthless, realistic and sinister foe that has infiltrated some of our key institutions.

October 4, 1952

We should think more of our faith in freedom and less of our fear of Communism.

February 14, 1959

. . . if the United States were to throw in the towel and come home and the Communists took over South Vietnam, then all over Southeast Asia, all over the Pacific, in the Mideast, in Europe, in the world . . .

March 22, 1971

Credibility:

All you have to do in this country is to tell the people the truth and not try to hide anything from them.

September 24, 1952

With regard to what you call the credibility gap . . . presidents, particularly when they have difficult problems in foreign affairs, inevitably are going to acquire some credibility gap.

March 22, 1971

America, The Beautiful?

America is a great nation. And America is great because her people are great.

August 8, 1968

The average person out there in New York, California, Florida, wherever he may live . . . is fed up with it [the government] . . . it costs too much, it doesn't work and he can't do anything about it.

March 21, 1971

Hooray for the Stumblebums:

The Truman-Acheson stumblebum policy caused the Korean War.

October 11, 1952

The decision to go into Korea was right. The Communists had to be stopped. President Truman deserves credit for making that decision.

September 6, 1953

There's No Line—but Don't Step Over It:

I have always opposed drawing a line because I know that the moment you draw a line that is an encouragement for the Communists to attack—to step up this blackmail and force you into a war you don't want.

September 21, 1960

We will not tolerate attacks which result in heavier casualties . . . . An appropriate response to these attacks will be made if they continue.

March 4, 1971

Make Nice to the Pinkos:

If we are going to talk color, I'd rather have good old American khaki than State Department pink.

October 9, 1952

I know that if that [peace] comes, it will only come because of the quality of our State Department personnel. I know that I can count on you . . . [for] the best advice of any chief executive of any nation in the world.

January 29, 1971

The Media—A Clear Critique:

It is time that our great newspapers have at least the same objectivity, the same fullness of coverage that television has. And I can only say thank God for television and radio for keeping the newspapers a little more honest.

November 17, 1962

I don't want to leave the impression that the pictures we have been seeing on television tell basically an inaccurate story. . . . But while a picture doesn't lie, a picture may not tell all the truth.

March 22, 1971

Thimk:

I remember going into my front room and sitting down and not saying anything or really thinking of anything for at least five or ten minutes.

September 24, 1956

What brings morale is not what happens in the ranks, but the leadership and example that is set at the top.

January 31, 1969

Self-Criticism:

Let's make sure that the side that wants peace has superiority over the side that wants expansion.

September 12, 1968

This is a time when belligerent talk could blow up the world.

September 12, 1968

I Am Number 1, Number 1, 1, 1, 1, 1, 1:

Yesterday, for the first time in history a man occupying the office of the President of the United States visited a session of the House of Commons.

February 26, 1969

This is the first time that I, as president of the United States, have appeared before any legislative body [Bundestag] in the whole world.

February 26, 1969

The first world capital I am visiting after greeting the first men on the moon is Manila.

July 26, 1969

As I stand here today, I realize for the first time in history a president of the United States is visiting Indonesia.

July 27, 1969

This is the first time I have ever said goodbye to the people of this country [Indonesia].

July 28, 1969

This is the first visit of a president of the United States to Rumania [and] the first state visit by an American president to a socialist country or to this region of the continent of Europe.

August 2, 1969

I am proud that, as president of the United States, the first welcome to a head of state [president of Korea] outside of Washington, D.C., is in my home state of California.

August 21, 1969

This is the first time in this administration we have had the honor to receive the head of government of another state who is also a woman [Golda Meir].

September 25, 1969

This is the first time in history that a president of the United States has ever spoken in Morris County.

October 29, 1969

To Know Him Is to——Him:

It is true that of all the presidents in this century, it is probably true, that I have less . . . supporters in the press than any president.

March 22, 1971, 10 P.M., EST

I have many friends in the press, personal friends.

March 22, 1971, 10:01 P.M., EST

Oh?

My [economic] policy has been described as moderation of partnership, the new capitalism, the people's capitalism or consumer capitalism.

September 23, 1956

Me, Complain?

I have no complaints about my press coverage.

November 8, 1962

And I say as I leave the press, all I can say is this: For sixteen years, ever since the Hiss case, you've had a lot of fun—*a lot of fun*—that you've had an opportunity to attack me.

November 8, 1962

Come to Me, My Thieving Baby:

We find embezzlement, thievery, knavery and criminal carelessness in American government.

October 3, 1952

The next president must unite America. He must calm its angers, ease its terrible frictions and bring people together once again in peace and mutual respect.

September 19, 1968

Now That's What I Call Hard Evidence:

It is also charged that Judge Carswell is a "racist." [However] a shipmate of Judge Carswell, who served with him aboard the U.S.S. *Baltimore* . . . describes Judge Carswell's attitude as "truly humanistic and liberal," and reports that he reacted to people without bias of race or color.

April 1, 1970

Equal Opportunity . . . Well, Almost:

The laws of society had to be changed so that doors could be opened to give everyone an equal chance on the starting line. . . . After ten years of opening doors we need a period of helping people walk through those doors.

January 13, 1968

When you say it is the responsibility of the federal government and the federal courts to carry out [school desegregation] and then use the power of the federal treasury to withdraw or give funds in order to carry it out, then I think we are going too far.

September 13, 1968

OPPORTUNITY

How to Produce More Arms and Less Weapons:

If elected president, I pledge to restore a clear-cut American military superiority over the Soviet Union.

October 24, 1968

The vast resources of the industrialized nations must be diverted from the non-productive and wasteful channels of war-making capabilities.

October 26, 1968

Contagious Morbidity:

Mr. Stevenson is morbidly preoccupied with troubles and disasters which he apparently thinks lurk behind every bush on the American scene.

October 18, 1956

The United States has become a lawless society.

May 8, 1968

Don't Hate Them—Love Me:

When crime has been going up nine times as fast as population, when there have been riots in three hundred cities, when the capital of this nation has become the crime capital of the world . . . then it is time to re-establish respect for the law.

September 21, 1968

Simply to allow Americans to vent their hatred as they vote for Nixon . . . that isn't enough.

October 18, 1968

A Hard Case:

Since it is easy to do, I don't know how to do it.

March 22, 1971

Don't Be an Island, I'll Build a Moat:

You can't be an island in the world. You can't live in your comfortable houses and say, "Well, just as long as I get mine, I don't have to worry about the others."

July 21, 1968

To force integration in the suburbs I think is unrealistic.

January 4, 1971

Do You Waive Consecutive Translation?

Third person, right. But you can use everything I say; everything is on the record. But if you could put it in the third person, that the president said that political clearances were not involved in the Supreme Court, then a reporter asks whether or not he had talked to the Chief Justice-Designate, and the president said that he talked to him for the first time, as I will indicate—like that.

May 22, 1969

With Friends Like Dick . . .

I indicated [to U Thant] our continuing support of the UN and our intention in these years ahead to do everything we can to strengthen the UN as it works in the cause of world peace.

December 18, 1969

In so far as those vital matters which affect their vital interests are concerned, the great powers will make their decisions. They will not submit those decisions to the UN for final action.

December 20, 1969

What a Difference a Few Years Can Make:

He [Stevenson] and his associates have attempted to capitalize on terror and fear to gain political advantage.

October 24, 1956

Some have said we are a sick society. We're sick all right, but not in the way they mean. We are sick of what has been allowed to go on in this nation for too long.

October 25, 1968

Technology, *Sí,* Technology, *No!*

The world of tomorrow belongs to the nations that lead in scientific research. We shall pay a great price if we fall behind in this contest.

June 7, 1956

It would be one of history's cruelest ironies if the American people should becomes slaves and victims of their own technological genius.

November 18, 1968

See Dick Run, See Jane Run:

I believe that at this time instead of talking only about and primarily about what is wrong about America, it is time to stand up and speak about what is right about America. Because, you see, what is right about America enables us to correct those things that are wrong about America. To do something, if I may borrow a phrase, about those things that are wrong.

June 24, 1970

Shucks, Twarn't Nothin':

Let me say that my service record was not a particularly unusual one. I went to the South Pacific. I guess I'm entitled to a couple of battle stars. I got a couple of letters of commendation. But I was just there when the bombs were falling.

September 20, 1952

Most leaders like to glamorize themselves.

November 17, 1962

Cause and Effect?

Pornographers actually buy and use the mailing lists of Cub Scouts.

October 9, 1968

I have found even in grade schools today, particularly in the sixth, seventh, and eighth grades, you will find a high degree of sophistication. . . .

February 7, 1969

Sometime Togetherness:

The great objective of this administration at the outset will be to bring the American people together.

September 6, 1968

I have reluctantly concluded, with the Senate as presently constituted, I cannot successfully nominate to the Supreme Court a federal appellate judge from the South who believes as I do in the strict construction of the Constitution.

April 9, 1971

Right On:

Good intentions and words are not enough.

October 31, 1956

I hope I can gain the respect and I hope eventually the friendship of black citizens and other Americans.

February 6, 1969

Give and Take:

This will be an administration open to new ideas of both parties, open to critics as well as those who support us.

November 6, 1968

There is nothing we can learn from [peace] demonstrations.

October 13, 1969

The Fable of the Vulture and the Cheshire Cat:

I say this: The boys in Korea never had it so bad.

October 11, 1952

He [Stevenson] gloats like a Cheshire cat over this turn in international events which is costing lives in the Middle East.

October 31, 1956

Who's Counting?

In my travels around the world, going back twenty-two years, in meeting American ambassadors in seventy-three countries . . .

February 25, 1969

I am the fourth president to receive you here in the White House.

July 8, 1969

I think I have visited fifty of the sixty countries represented here.

July 22, 1969

This is the third time I have said goodby at this airport.

July 28, 1969

Your Majesty, this is the sixth time I have visited your country.

July 28, 1969

As I leave India after this third visit . . .

August 1, 1969

It is a special pleasure for me to return on this, my sixth visit.

August 1, 1969

This is the ninth time over the past twenty years that Your Majesty has honored our country.

October 21, 1969

This is your third visit to the United States.

November 19, 1969

In this one-hundredth anniversary of football . . . both of them I wish could be Number One. But at the end, which ever is Number One will deserve it, and the Number Two team . . .

December 6, 1969

Now in just seventy years . . . as we enter the decade of the '70s we have 200 million people and, by the end of the century, just thirty-five years more, thirty years more, we will be 300 million people.

December 16, 1969

This is the fourth occasion on which I visited the North American College.

September 28, 1970

Strength Through Weakness:

The American economy is the strongest in the world.

June 6, 1970

Unemployment has increased, the price index continues to rise, profits have gone down, the stock market has declined, interest rates are too high.

June 6, 1970

Boy, Can They Go Backwards:

In the south of Indochina, the Communists have moved out and we have a strong free bastion there.

October 13, 1960

In that six weeks' period the South Vietnamese have developed a considerable capability on their own and considerable confidence on their own. They are better units to handle the situation as we withdraw.

March 22, 1971

Practically All Life Is Precious:

Now as far as Quemoy and Matsu are concerned . . . the few people who live on them they are not too important.

October 7, 1960

The death of a single man in war, whether he's American, South Vietnamese, Vietçong or North Vietnamese is a human tragedy.

April 20, 1970

Running Standing Still:

For us deliberately to let a weaker, but basically expansionist nation achieve [arms] parity indicates an erosion of our commitment and will.

October 24, 1968

If elected, I pledge to seek meaningful arms control agreements with our adversaries.

October 26, 1968

How to Win Friends:

This [91st] Congress will be remembered and remarked upon in history, not so much for what it did, but what it did not do . . . . In probably no month in recent history did the reputation of the whole Congress suffer more in the eyes of the American people, than in December 1970.

January 5, 1971

I respect Congress . . . I would like a better understanding in the Congress.

March 22, 1971

Surprise!

I would be very much surprised to learn that a decision involving national security was made or not made on the basis of political consideration.

October 10, 1956

He [Johnson] is a skillful operator. He uses the power of the federal government, at times ruthlessly, to serve political ends.

February 18, 1968

Jumping the Gun:

I have consistently answered all questions with regard to who will be in the next cabinet by saying that is the responsibility of the next president and it would be inappropriate to make any decision on that . . . prior to the time that I had a right to do so.

October 21, 1956

And if we are to restore respect for law and order in this country, there's one place we're going to begin: we're going to have a new attorney general of the United States.

August 8, 1968

The Gentle Art:

Because, you see, the art of preserving peace is greater than that of waging war.

August 8, 1968

It will be my policy as president to issue a warning only once, and I will not repeat it now. Anything in the future that is done will be done. There will be no additional warning.

March 3, 1969